Stock Market Investing For Beginners:

Discover The Easiest way For Anyone to Retire a Millionaire and Build Passive Income with Only 10 Hours Work or less per year Through The Stock Market

By

Victor Adams

Disclaimer

All contents provided in this book is to inform and to instruct the reader from the author's selected perspective. Therefore, the author is free from any responsibility taken for any results or outcomes resulting from the use of this material. However, conscious effort has been made to make sure that all information provided is accurate and effective. Note that the author would not be blamed for any misuse or misrepresentation of information.

Table of Contents

Before You Start Investing

Well, it is logical to learn to invest before you start some real investment. Maybe a course in investing 101 should be compulsory or mandated. However, here is a story about a very good friend of mine. In the dean's office one of the largest universities in America, he asked if there was a course titled investing 101 or personal investment. He didn't get that answer then. The fact is that someday we would start investing money and it would be a battle between the informed vs. uninformed. There are over 50,000 students throughout a university who have enrolled in Thousands of courses, but you can't find a course talking about investing or investment. I am not canvassing for the change of curriculum I am just stating the fact that what you are going to read here is not going to be taught in universities. Meaning that it would be a long while before this becomes something exposed to everyone.

Before you jump into different financial concepts like asset allocation and strategy, things you already know you should understand the basics: investment characteristics and how to evaluates all other options that are available to you, till you determine what you want and stick to it. You should match your financial wants and needs to the various options and get the best process which suits you and your personal investing goals. There is no single best choice for a financial goal; there are several options you should explore until you get the best. However, what you do is to take your time and consider understanding the basics before you decide to pick one. Whether you are an investor or not, you should understand the basics of investment. Once you've been able to understand those financial concepts you can start investing with confidence. Once you learn how to invest properly, you can reach your financial goals which so much ease. The largest university in the world is the one having no school walls.

Investing comes down to some few basic principles, and without these principles, you shouldn't think or even try to invest. What drives me sometimes is that power to pick the best stock and to buy it. As an investor, you deserve reliable information and instruction so that you can craft out that investment strategy which would fit your need. The first thing is to get that feel for numbers. Research is very subjective, and the analysts offer several options and make estimates for a particular stock. I center all the basics around these eight key fundamental principles; Increasing sales, Expanding Operating Margins, Free Cash Flow, Earnings Growth, Positive Earning Momentum and Return on Equity. All these eight fundamentals would help you discover the best stocks to buy on Wall Street or anywhere. There are several websites where you can get this information and even participate in virtual stock instantly so that you'll know what is perfect for you.

Furthermore, you should also learn to focus on the future. Don't dwell on the past mistakes and you shouldn't get too caught up in the anxious act of checking prices every hour. The long term performance of any stock or investment should be your motivation and concentration. I've had my share of bad days, but I tell you that the bad days cannot be compared with the benefits I have gotten from the good days. The truth is that; what happened in the last market cycle won't necessarily apply to the next so you shouldn't lose sight of the broad market when you are thinking of investing. Furthermore, you should learn to diversify and keep on diversifying. You should have a diversified portfolio as an investor. That is because a diversified portfolio is that mix of dozens of stocks which in several different investment areas yield stronger, steadier and would possess less risk. And in the long run, if some of your investments perform poorly, then your big gainers will neutralize all your losses. Going with the same principle, you should learn to take *partial profits* in several companies; this means that you should make sure that a single stock never becomes too big for your portfolio. You can sell a portion of your holdings while you keep enough stock to continue to cash in if the ride hasn't ended. More also, you should always sell into strength. The simple principle is buying low and selling high. That is easier said than done right? Well, not really. Well, you should learn to sell something in any position you find yourself and make sure you are able to make a lot of profit from it. So it is advisable that you don't wait too long. Take your chances and make those calculated risk.

You should also expect volatility. You should not be afraid of big market swings especially because they can profit you. Learn how to deal with volatility. This means that you should be able to make money even in the most topsy-turvy market environments. Most of the time I'll advise that you should stick to the 60-30-10 rule which means that 60% of your portfolio must be in the most conservative stocks then 30% should be in the moderately aggressive stocks while 10% should be in the aggressive stocks. What happens when you have this mix? Well, it gives you that smooth path to profits over that long run. The market is volatile, and this mix keeps the portfolio afloat.

This chapter will not be complete if we fail to talk about *trusting your gut.* The truth is that there is no good investment strategy; things change so you should trust yourself. Don't think that one investing strategy is all wrong just because it doesn't sync well with what the latest guru on Wall Street says or because it is not in line with the weekly report. And who says that you can't create your own strategy? Be open-minded. Open yourself up to those intricacies and create your own principle. That is one of the best ways to grow as an investor.

Debt-The Life Destroyer

Debt is truly a life destroyer. The problem is that it keeps getting bigger and bigger and more people continue to find themselves in that trap every day.It's like the older you get, the bigger it becomes. But why is this happening? Or what is the problem? We find it hard to know how so many individuals can let themselves get into this situation without even knowing it. First, we have to trace the root of the problem. The biggest cause of debt as it stands now is the availability of credit card! But it is a credit card. Yes, definitely. It says credit card, but it is the number one debt accumulator.

The problem is that everywhere you go you see several offers for money, loans and all kinds of cards. This availability is considered the problem. The worst thing is that it becomes very easy to owe multiple sources. You might have a home loan, a car loan, and even some unsecured personal loans. You may have that store of cards, and you'll be wondering when you are going to be able to pay it up.

For the simple fact that it is very easy to get credit card, most individuals misuse this opportunity. They fall into that life of debt from the very beginning and could remain like that for the rest of their lives. But have you ever wondered how? Well, it starts with those free offers you see from retail shops. Then it would encourage you to spend more money than you want to. Furthermore, they make their offers so exciting that you wouldn't want to turn it down. I remember one day when I was offered this bait. I walked into a store, and I was curious. I checked the APR it was so enticing enough. They offered an astounding 39.9%, and they would definitely give you 20% off your first purchase. If you fail to pay it back all at once (which is what they pray for) you'll end up paying them 3 times more!

It is possible to have multiple sources of debt, and it becomes a huge problem when you combine all of it, you have a large and unmanageable level of debt. The truth remains that when you are trying to *balance* your credit, you find out that you are not making any significant progress because you are only covering your interest charges. Take a look at your credit card statement this month. Is it looking good? Check your monthly payment and check how much interest was added. Are the figures shocking right? Well, that is you and all your bad spending habits on a piece of paper. What's worse is that debt is becoming a way of life, and it is getting ingrained in our culture, and this explains why most people simply accept all terms and conditions given, maybe because they assume that the contract is 'right' and they can actually control it. However, that is not the case. Most people don't even know what APR they are paying on their credit cards. All this information shouldn't be strange to you as an investor. These persons fail to understand the significance of each step they make. When you get a credit card, you are essentially signing that contact or that legal commitment of earning and paying that set amount each month. Note that it is not savings. It would be fine if you are able to keep to this commitment, but problems would occur which would stretch you, and in this situation, you would be expected to pay up as your interest rate begin to rise. The bigger problem would be that sudden issues like unemployment would cause legal issues because of the first mistake of putting down your signature during your disposition.

Debt creeps on you all of a sudden. First, we are happily going about our daily lives, not paying too much attention to our spending. Then we just pop it on the credit card. After all, it is just some few dollars.

The car needs servicing, the kids want new trainers, and the list keeps going on forever. But that is not a problem until when one day it dawns on you, and you'll be like; *what? When did I spend this much? How did I arrive at this balance?* You are surprised at first when you apply for additional cards. Then you start the cycle once more with more available credit. Then that quick check of all your balances at the back of the envelope. Boom, you're surprised once more.

Then you would discover that you can't even meet up with the minimum payments on time. What's next? You apply for a personal loan to consolidate all the credit and store card balances into that easy and affordable monthly payment just the way they tell you. You have just succeeded in robbing Peter to Paul. The only problem here is that you are not robbing, but you are borrowing. Well, you think everything is fine, and you have nothing to worry about right? That is just a façade they want you to believe.

It only comes crashing down, and the minimum payment would become something you can't meet up to again. Then you scream for help! And you start to get financial advice from the *experts*. Well, Bankruptcy is the last resort not the end of the world, it allows you to start again with that clean state although obtaining future credit after this initial discharge would become very difficult.

Now, this leads us to the question of the century: *can we live a debt-free life?* It is like asking if someone can survive without a credit card because it is becoming a necessity gradually. My answer is simple. You can live a debt-free life. Yes, it is possible. This is not something from the abstract world or a statement to motivate you; I would back it up with facts. Because it wouldn't flow well to tell you the dangers of something without providing steps on how to eliminate or stop its negative effects.

Let me arouse your interest. Do you know that an individual can possibly save up to $1,000,000 and eliminate all debt they can pay off their mortgage by investing in that safe mutual funds? Credit isn't expected to be all good. In fact, credits are not in the creditor's best interest. However, you can make use of that magic input. The magic input is the amount that you set aside to pay extra bills in that specific sequence. There are sites which can help you do this or you can do this manually, and you'll get tremendous results.

- First, you will go to your last six to seven months of check register then you would list items which you hope to reduce. Note that bills shouldn't be inclusive because they would soon be paid off, taxes, etc. are facts of life.

- Make sure you categorize each entry into several segments. Like groceries, lunches, savings, entertainment, etc.

- Sit down and think of ideas on how you can save on all these items you've listed making sure that you arrive at a 10% total gross. For example, if an item costs $90 you should devise a means of making it cost $80 or even less. But don't forget that it is temporary so you don't need to start so big.

After you have been able to do this successfully what is next for you is to start the Payoff Sequence. The payoff sequence is quite complex but not difficult when you follow the right principles.

1. Make sure you divide the total payoff amount by the monthly payment. Make sure you pick that numeric sequence which starts with 1 for that lowest division.

2. For every month the normal monthly payment to each debt should be made. You should repeat this process until the debt is fully paid.

3. You should pay the minimum monthly bills except the debt two. What this means is that you pick each debt one after the other for each month. You don't just pay little

by scattering your little resources around, it wouldn't have any value, and the interest would continue to add up.

4. One thing I am sure this method would teach you is how to control spending, and it would also make you realize that you are spending your money on some useless items and you would need to change that.

The major concept here is to pay off the interest of your small debts first before you use the money as leverage to pay up the rest. First,you face the initial concept of picking your debt or debt selection, and you should agree to pay the one with the biggest interest first. Employing this method shows that you are ready to get out of debt and you are ready to do it quick.

Well, most of the time there are three questions that come to the minds of those who find themselves in debt. First is how did I get here? Why is this happening to me? And how am I going out of this? A pile of debt can bring so much onerous burden. It can also bring a great number of psychological problems also. However, if you take the right step, you would be able to avoid it. Quickly, I would share some steps;

First, you should question every buying. You should ask yourself a number of question about every purchase you are about to make. Do you actually need that item or it is just a want? If you put off the purchase for a while would it affect you negatively? You shouldn't be battling against debt while you continue to accommodate its problem. Sometimes asking these questions would break some bad spending habits. Next, you should keep a fixed amount which you plan to spend on expenses each week. If you plan on buying something which would make you exceed that fixed amount, you should cancel that plan. You should make it of great necessity to give precedence to your expenditure. It should be what you need and not what you want. Furthermore, it is not bad if you go 'low-priced' there is nothing bad in telling yourself that; *I can't afford this*. You shouldn't carry along that mentality of *letting me get it even though I would suffer for it.* You should go low-priced and even get non-branded equivalents instead of the items which are very expensive but popular. Shop around for the best prices; this would help you to lower your cost drastically. And when you lower your cost, you'll be able to save money.

Conclusively, you should have a spending plan and stick to it. I know this can be very hard. Fighting that urge to buy something that you really like or because you cannot just get something that you love because you are on a budget. But I tell you that a comfortable life free of debt is better than an extravagant life sinking in the ocean of debt. After paying all your bills and buying the necessity which you need personally or in your household do you have some money left? That spending plan would help you get the right answer to that. The spending plan is just a simple word for the budget. Don't get confused. Remember that the first thing for you to do is to prioritize your needs, create that spending strategy and adjust your finances to the best of your interest. If you fail to do that by ignoring your spending decision and not keeping to the fixed amount that you are to spend per week, it leads to overspending immediately which can lead you into that life of debt. Poor planning or having no plan at all is another factor which can lead to financial problems like debt. Debt is a life destroyer, don't allow it destroy you.

Avoiding Bad Credit

It is important that we should know the causes of bad credit as credit can be a tricky thing. A quick list of what we are going to discuss in this chapter includes; paying late or not at all, maxing out your card, closing credit accounts, etc.

Having said that, below is a comprehensive list of the cause of bad credit in no particular order:

Missing Payments: We don't need a credit expert to tell us that missing payments is a bad thing for your credit history, credit score and overall, your finances. You should know by now credit scores look at your credit history to see how you have been able to manage your current and past credit obligations in order to predict how likely it's going to be for you to miss payments in the future. When you miss payments, you predict the future that you are going to miss more and more payments. It's like your past and even your present, form your future. There are several ways missing payments could severely damage your credit score some of them are;

- How frequently you pay late: For someone who misses payments very frequently, he/she would be penalized more severely than someone who misses payments infrequently. The trick is this; even if you want to miss payments, something you shouldn't don't make it too often.

- How serious are your late payments: You may be *fashionably late* or *completely late.* The difference between both has to do with the time duration. You should know that the severity of your late payment plays a trivial part in your credit score and contributes to your credit history as well. For someone who missed a payment by only a few weeks and brought his/her payment up to date is likely to have a score better than someone whose payment is 90 days overdue or worse. When you have late payments make sure you do all you can to bring them up to date as soon as possible, it's for your own good.

- How current is your late payment: We are aware that the scoring models are designed to forecast how you will pay your bills in future if you keep paying late your credit score depreciates drastically too. For someone having his late payments more often in the last two years would definitely missa payment in the next two years than an individual having no late payments.

Closing Credit Card Accounts: Closing credit card is as bad as missing payments or even worse, you may be wondering how this is possible. But let me tell you that closing credit card account doesn't boost your credit scores; it does the opposite. Closing your credit card account is the most common piece of misguided counsel an individual would receive when he/she asks how the credit score can be increased. Many have fallen victim of this wrong advice, and I would give you some reasons why closing credit cards accounts wouldn't increase your credit score.

First, a closed account will definitely reflect on your credit report earlier than opening a new one. Coupled with that, credit reporting agencies, banks, and lenders would have to follow specific rules which depend on how long the new information would remain on your credit report. Most times, negative credit information would stain your credit report or remain in your credit files for seven years from the date the first debt became neglected. While positive credit information can remain indefinitely, on the other hand, closed accounts in good standing are most times removed from the credit report within ten years after closing! Surprised? That's not all. As soon as the credit score starts deriving its value from the progressive history which is related to an account but the owner decides to close the account, the good report is gone- totally removed from the report when that account is removed. The "good history" of how you had been faithful for years with your credit is gone in an instant, and sadly such history would remain untraceable once you close the credit card account. Yeah, you may be thinking *is this really bad? A credit score favors a long credit history, isn't it? Because the length of my credit history accounts for 15% of a FICO score right?* You should know that individuals with a fresh or young credit card history are usually seen as more risky borrowers than those who have credit for many years. You should hang onto those old accounts if you can by making sure they remain open. Make sure you do all you can to keep them open, closing them may look very simple and easy, but its negative footprints may be hard to leave your credit record. That is why you need to think twice before you open any credit account.

Another thing closing credit card account does to you is that it hurts your "utilization" measurements. In the short run, this is considerably more important than your closed accounts diminishing from your credit reports. Revolving utilization is a terminology used to refer to the revolving credit card limits that are in use on your credit card. It is called revolving because it changes all the time. For example, if you have an open credit account having $3000 as your credit limit and a $1500 balance, you are 50% "utilized" on that particular account, obviously because you are using half of your credit limit. This particular scaling makes up to 30% of your credit score. And has the same importance as making your payments on time on your credit score. As this particular percentage increases, your credit score also decreases. You must have noticed that the issue of credit is not as simple as you think it is, there is no need to worry so long you understand the simple rudiments which are in this book. Having given you a little detail about "utilization measurements," we would need to further our knowledge

Over-Utilization of Available Credit Card Limits: Just as we have mentioned that high balances on your credit cards increase the chances of your credit score going low, over-utilization can become a big problem. Now I know what you might be thinking, why do I have a limit of $3000 when I can't use up to that amount? From now on, I want you to look at your limit, not as a "limit" per se but a gauge. A place you should never reach. If by chance you happen to be in this position over utilizing your available credit card limits, your best bet would be to use your cards scarcely or in moderation. You should try your best to reduce that percentage as much as possible, and then your score would gradually work its way back up. It is safe to say that the lower the percentage, the better it becomes as there is no special target to shoot at. It all depends on you. I would like you to take this as a rule: you should not reach your credit card limit. Restrain yourself from excessive buying.

Settling with your lender or credit company on past due to account: settling is when your credit industry or lender accepts an amount which is less than the actual amount you owe on an account. Take, for example, you owe a credit card company $15,00, but some "unforeseen" circumstances couldn't allow you to pay that amount in full, a deal for less than that full amount would be made. Once that deal is accepted by both parties then we can say a "settling" exists. This sounds like a good idea isn't it? You are not to pay the full amount, what a relief.

Nonetheless, the lender will account for that remaining amount to the credit bureau as a negative item. The outstanding amount is called the "deficiency balance." This deficiency balance is seen as a negative scoring model just as the credit bureaus see severe late payments. A smart option exists for you here; if you can make it possible to arrange a deal with your lender so that he wouldn't report the deficiency balance. If you can come to an agreement then what is left is that you should find a way to pay in full or you may face the consequences for 7 years.

Excessively Shopping for Credit: shopping for credit here means; filling out several credit application. Let me tell you what happens. Filling out a credit application means that you are giving the lender license to access your credit reports. After accessing your credit reports, automatically they post an "inquiry." This inquiry is a history profile or note of who pulled your credit report and the date also. The federal law states that the inquiry remains on the report for the period of 24 months.

Nevertheless, credit scores only look at inquiries which are less than a year old. These inquiries are utilized by credit scoring models in order to determine whether or not an individual is shopping for credit or not. These inquiries are utilized by credit scoring models to decide whether or not someone is shopping for credit. It remains the fact that consumers or individuals with more inquiries attract higher credit risk than those with fewer inquiries. These means that the more you make queries and investigations about your credit the more points you lose. Isn't that ridiculous?.Excessively shopping for credit doesn't only attract the attention of lenders to produce inquiries it reduces your credit scores, damages your history and could also destroy your financial life if you're not cautious enough.

Having the thought that all credit scores are the same: We would discuss more of this when we are talking about Credit score in the next chapter. However, we need to understand little for now. Nothing should make us think that all credit scores are the same. This is one mistake individuals make, and it also gets confusing. There are different types of credit score just as there are different types of soft drinks. We shouldn't take one kind of credit score like the other just as we can't take 7up as Coca-Cola. There are several places where consumers could purchase credit reports and credit scores, but not all scores sold are similar. Coming upon this nugget of information may sound normal or easy to you making it irrelevant, but I tell you that if you fail to take this into consideration, your credit score may suffer. A very good example comes to mind here. If you want to purchase a new car and you buy an "educational" (car sold to consumers, but not used by lenders) or another type of credit score which is premature for your own information. The score you would receive would be definitely different from the score the borrower is looking at. Every borrower, bank or credit company has separate lending standards. A particular credit score may earn you a good deal from one lender but not from another.

Having the thought that all credit scores forecast the same thing: Knowing this, may add to the confusion from the last point but know that we would rectify this in the next chapter, for now,there are models which predict other things than general credit risk. For the scoring models, they can be forecasted or predicted on almost anything which includes all or some of the following:

- Insurance Risk: Yes, insurance risk greatly affects and predicts your credit score. It is no new news that most insurance companies utilize credit scoring models to predict whether or not you are liable to file an auto or homeowner's insurance claim. Any poor insurance score could mean that you will pay higher premiums.

- Revenue Potential: Credit card companies aim to generate revenue not to lend out money for lending sake. Your revenue scoring models could be used by credit card companies to calculate or foretell whether or not you will use their credit card and most importantly create more revenue for them.

- Response Rates: Sometimes, you would check your mail and then you would see "pre-approved" offers of credit. This is no coincidence, and it is not just something sent randomly. The real deal is that you have been selected from several millions of other individuals to receive that offer due to the fact that you have a "Response Score" which shows that you are more likely to reply to such an offer than anyone else.

- Collectability: Some individuals have collections as part of their credit report. This means that collection agencies are assigned to accumulate the past due debts and thereby to score you to decide whether or not you are likely to reimburse your collection debt sooner than others.

- Fraud Potential: These scoring models have become so sophisticated that they can actually predict whether or not you are trying to make a fraudulent purchase with your credit card. The most surprising thing or amazing thing about this is that it takes just a few minutes to check-out at a store, but within these short amount of time, the serious calculation is going on because you may have been scored to see whether the retailer should accept your credit card or not.

- Bankruptcy potential: The bankruptcy scores hypothesize the chances that you will file for personal bankruptcy. Having a poor bankruptcy score can cause your credit applications to be declined. You may think being bankrupt happens to companies and individuals who own businesses. Well, the ugly head of bankruptcy could show itself on the financial aspect of every individual. And when you have the potential to "become broke" at any given time, no credit card company, loaner or bank would want to give you funds.

When you don't understand your right under the fair credit reporting act: The "FCRA," as it is usually called is a list of credit reporting regulations and rules which direct lenders as well as credit reporting agencies. As a credit conscious individual, you should become familiar with your rights and also the "permissible purposes" as well under which your credit reports can be viewed. You have rights to dispute errors on your credit reports-we would talk about that later, and you also have right to a free copy of your credit reports from each of the three credit reporting agencies. These are your rights, and it is very important that you should know them.

When you fail to realize that you have 3 credit reports and equivalent Credit Scores: Most individuals have the understanding that a credit report exists. But they don't know that an individual has three credit reports which are successfully compiled and maintained by three independent competing companies known as the "credit reporting agencies." These companies store your credit history and even sell them to lenders and consumers likewise. The three largest are; Experian, TransUnion, and Equifax. Each credit report is used to calculate many different credit scores so you should not be on the assuming side that your credit report and scores are all similar.

How To Never Worry About Life's Chaos Again

Well, you wouldn't need to worry about life's chaos if you have enough in the bank. But the most surprising thing is that even when individuals stumble upon a huge sum of money or even win a lottery after some few months, they are back to how they were before. Well, the process is quite simple. First, they start by *enjoying my life* strategy. Not really a strategy but a principle. An inherent principle entrenched to the minds of those who have that poverty mentality. A modern person should invest 50% of his/her income but what happens is that we find it hard to save and harder to invest because you would use what you have to get more. It is safe and true to say that savings would fetch you more money, but we both know that we only save to have that extra money to spend when unplanned needs arise.

Sometimes when we have so many funds that wouldn't need us to worry about life's chaos again, we squander all of it and our rat race resumes. In this chapter, you would be exposed to the power of savings. Yes, I am aware that you know what savings are all about, you have probably read *Rich Dad, Poor Dad* by Robert Kiyosaki or any other popular book. I am sure you are aware of the fact that savings can push you from poverty to wealth. However, what happens is that we have that goal, but it never comes into fruition. Let me explain the simple process of how we dump all knowledge into that recessive mind of ours. You read a book about savings. You are inspired. *Oh, I want to start saving, yes, I really need to do something.* The book goes further to provide you with enough strategies to help you. You finish the book, and you are excited. *Let's start saving!* The first month, you struggle to save some money. The second month becomes harder than the first. Next, something comes up, and you use all your savings for it. *Oh, no! This is not what I planned for.* Then you start all over again. *I must do this. I really need to do this.* You save for three months consecutively and again you make use of the funds for something else. Then you give up. You literarily don't care anymore. *This is impossible; let's live life the way it should be, not worrying about tomorrow.* Yes, it is true that you shouldn't worry about tomorrow, but those who prepare and plan for the future always find themselves in the best situations. Yes, plans may fail but when you shoot for the stars, you can end up reaching the moon, and that is not bad also. When the rainy day comes what should you do? Keep some, spend some, spend some and spend what you've kept in the future because you're broke. The truth is that most people have that saving mentality. We want to save, but we find it hard to do so.

Every month, you dream of spending just a little bit of money in your budget and taking that second honeymoon or vacation. After making all those plans and fantasizing about them, you wouldn't have enough money to make them a reality. When people think of financial planning, they place savings for retirement or emergencies at the forefront only to relegate it later on. While these are essential to ensuring that you never face that financial ruin, having a rainy day fund can and must be very important for unexpected situations which are short term in nature and those little dreams would become possible.

Starting to save for a rainy day is not rocket science. You should just understand some familiar principles and put them into practice. First, you should understand that *a little goes a long way.* If your car breaks down today, would you have extra cash on hand to fix it? The fact remains that when most individuals start saving for that rainy day they become discouraged and the funds wouldn't be for the rainy day any longer but for any use. Most times we think that we need to contribute that large sum of money to savings every day. That is the first mistake we make. We don't need to go big. Just start small. That small portion from each check you get can go a long way. Make every day count and make every week count also. As long as you are consistent you'll be fine.

The next thing to do is to automate your savings. Most employers would be happy to help save for that rainy day if you ask them to do so. If you have that right paperwork filled out, you would be able to arrange it. When your savings is automated, you would be able to reach your goals at all cost. Most times you wouldn't even know the difference after your savings has been deducted because you would be building your budget on your current income and you wouldn't know when you begin to cut cost. Furthermore, it is ideal for you to contribute to windfalls. In the sense that it would be difficult for you to spend that unexpected money which is not related to your income or savings, things like a bonus, tax return or maybe a birthday gift. That urge to spend it should be suppressed. Place it in your savings account immediately.

A rainy day fund serves two major purposes. First, it helps you prepare for that short term financial crises, and it also provides you with that opportunity to live your dreams also. Creating a budget is also a good way to achieve this. Even on your phone, you can create a budget. There are several software which could help you with that. Creating your budget shouldn't be the problem but following it would always prove challenging. The best way to start saving for that rainy day is, to begin with, automated savings, using windfalls and taking advantage of several online saving tools just like budgeting software, etc.

Experts claim that you should have anywhere between three to six months' expenses saved up as an emergency fund. Well, I would agree with that because the more you have been able to save up, the more secure you would feel when an emergency comes your way.

Creating an extra source of income is also a good way to get that rainy day fund. Think of it this way that the more money you have, the more money you can save. When you are in the business world, the best way to save is to input money into several operations. The beauty about this is that you don't save only; your money keeps working for you. *Are we getting near investment?* Yes. Maybe.

It is not hard or complicated to figure out how you spend your money. You understand math to a certain degree, and you understand how to follow a budget. Now, it is a nice idea if you can do this yourself instead of getting someone. *Wait, do people get others to help draft out their personal budget?* Well, doing it yourself makes you understand how best the number works. You'll know what is going on instead of you to assume what is going on and you'll be able to create that perfect set up for yourself. Tracking what goes out and what comes in is the ground process of any business in this world. When you understand that there is actually much value to your time, you wouldn't want to spend it reading so many printouts or piles of document *(if your business requires you to do so)* but instead you would begin to concern yourself with the process of budgeting making the right rows for the months and the columns for the income as well as expenses. This principle works for personal use as well as corporate use. However, in the business world, you would have a very complex budget still based on the fundamental principles of budgeting. The fundamentals would have a column for; Gross revenue: where your money is coming from then expenses; where your money is going followed by the Net income: how much I left for you.

Taking a look at what you have, you should understand that the key is to make every expense accountable and measurable also. You should figure out which expenses are essential and the ones that are not. Learn to cut the fat. Your budget should be placed in a place where you can see it daily. Revisit it regularly and make a weekly meeting to visit your *team* to review the business process for that week. The twenty minutes you spend reviewing your budget could save you twenty thousand in the future.

Hefty expenses occur all the time. You may need a new car, a bigger house or you may just decide to go back to school to get your degree. How do people who find themselves in this situation react? The first thing they do is to go into debt once again. If you have a budget, this shouldn't be a problem because funds from a rainy day would help you. If you don't have a budget, then you are spending without thinking. Yes, read that again because when you become broke in the middle of the month, you wouldn't be able to track your expenses. Okay, you may be thinking; *I have a budget, but I find it very hard to stick with it.* Well, that happens because you don't understand how budgeting can improve your financial life. If you do understand how important it is to keep that budget, you would protect it and stick to it at all cost. However, if you are struggling with sticking to your budget, I would provide you with some few strategies.

First, you should focus on your savings. *Aren't we tired of talking about savings?* No, because it is very important. Make saving money a priority in your life. When you create your budget using that your personal finance software, you should learn to cut cost to save each month and set aside some funds from your paycheck. The surprising thing about savings is that it doesn't depend on how much you are earning but how much you are willing to save. Some might be earning millions but find it hard to save some while some might be earning hundreds, but they have that saving culture. *Okay, they are saving because they are broke.* If you go with this perception, you are completely wrong. *He who is faithful over little would be faithful when it comes to having that big task.* Those having little plus a good saving culture would have easy lives when they start earning big.

Furthermore, you should learn to use cash. Stay away from credit cards. Don't just walk into a store to make a purchase using a credit card. When you are using cash, you would understand how important savings is because just seeing the paper leaving your hands is enough to force you to save, especially when it is your hard-earned currency. You should learn to take a certain amount of cash out of your account each week which you would spend on gas, food and those extra expenses might not be needed all the time.

Another step you can take to stick to your budget is to cut out the bad habits. While you may be enjoying drinking, smoking, partying or just having fun you shouldn't make an expensive lifestyle become a habit. Learn to cut out bad habits. Yes, it is good to live large if you can afford it. If you can't, leave the Gucci Shoes and bags for now. When you are financially stable enough, you'll get them. Don't go broke trying to be rich. You don't need to be who you are not. Sharing your budgeting responsibilities isn't a bad idea also. It would help you stick to it. You may have a roommate or a family. Spending habits should be monitored. You should learn to stop spending money haphazardly. Sit down and wok out that budget together with your family, friend your personal finance software and even your entire household.

Save $1000 in a month.

Let us tell the truth. Americans suck at saving money. Not only Americans though Africans, Asians and citizens of the world in general. Most times, we really don't know how to identify the long term investment goals and satisfy them. Instead, we go into debt and heap the blame on every other person because we don't see what is wrong in borrowing money or spending excessively. The truth is that we want to know how to save money, but we don't want to really save money. We care less about proper asset allocation, and we don't want to bother ourselves about the stock market returns. All we just care about is the money we have right now. The #save $1000 a monthis put together not to provide that stupid frugal tips but to expose you to that life of savings and the benefits of putting money away for a while. Why start with something big? Or why jump into this idea? First, saving $1 per week or $10 per week is cool. However, it is not challenging, and it is not worth changing your behavior. Yes, if you really want to change something. Make it big! So that the difference can be obvious. Saving $1000 in 30 days is okay, it is big, and when the results come, you'll find out that you've not just wasted your time, but you've been able to accomplish something great. You should start this only if you're serious.

If or when you save $1000 a month you would have $12,000 in a year. In 20 years you would have $240,000 if you are just saving alone, nothing else. However, do you know that if you invest your savings in the sixth or even in the third month, you can become a millionaire in the space of three years while you are still keeping those savings of yours?Yes, it is possible. Let's do that quick math. During the sixth month, you would have $6000. If you invest that amount, you can be receiving interest of $1000 every month *if you play your cards right.* You would gain an extra $12000 from investment in one year. The beauty about investment is that you can start small, get big and still continue until it becomes bigger and bigger. You can make use of the part in the $12,000 to invest, or you put in all of it. With the proper stock, you can get up to $54,000 in a year. Multiply that amount by 10 (ten years) you'll get $540,000 in ten years. It wouldn't be smart of you if you wait till you have $540,000 before investing again you can make use of the $54,000 and gain $648,000 in a year. Multiply that amount by just two years. You'll have $1,296,000. Convinced?

The secret to investing is to forget that your money is someone else working for you. It may be hard and not easy I tell you but after you place that investment you'll never regret it. Saving is a huge step towards financial freedom and investment is one of the best ways to become rich beyond your thinking in a short while. Furthermore, you should learn to hold yourself capable of your incompetence.

Stock Market Terminologies

You are a beginner, that is cool because even the experts were once like you. Having said that, it would be inconsiderate of me if I fail to speak or relate to your own level of knowledge. That is why this chapter was just chipped in so that you can understand all the jargons. We are aware that the stock market is simply an exchange that gives people that opportunity and space to purchase and sell stocks. Well, the stock exchange is just buying and selling in disguise. I would list some terminologies which I think would be very helpful.

1. Annual report. The annual report is what a company presents which contains information about the company and its cash flow. The funny thing here is that annual

report isn't meant for stock market alone.

2. Averaging Down. As an investor, you may decide to buy more of a stock as the price goes down. This means that the amount you use in purchasing, your average purchasing decreases. People do this when they expect that the stock would rebound later.

3. Beta: This is the relationship between the price of a stock and the movement of the market. A market moves. It is either things are getting cheaper or costlier. So let us say if stock XYZ has a beta of 1.5 what this means is that stock XYZ has a beta of 1.5

4. Broker: A broker is an individual who sells an investment for you and receives a commission.

5. Dividend is a part of the company's earnings that are paid to shareholders, or those individuals who own that company's stock. It is paid on a quarterly or annual basis.

6. Index. The index is what is used as that citation or reference marker for investors. Portfolio managers would also take a good look at the index before thinking of managing your stock. Popular examples are the Standard & Poor's 500 and Dow Jones Industrial Average.

7. Portfolio: The portfolio is a collection of investments which is owned by an investor and makes up his/her portfolio. However, you can have an infinite amount of stocks and even other securities.

8. Volatility: this has to do with the price of a stock or the stock market as an entity. Stocks that are highly

volatile are those who are extreme and have daily up and down movements. Stocks that are considered volatile are Stocks that are delicate and carefully traded. They also have low trading volumes.

9. Moving average: A stock's average price per share which is used during that specific period of time is known as the moving average. You should be able to study some common time frames of study which has to do with terms of a stock's moving average which includes 50 and 200-day moving averages.

10.   Close. The NYSE and Nasdaq closed at 4 p.m., but the after-hours trading would continue until 8 p.m. the close just means that there is a time which a stock exchange closes to trading.

Introduction To The Stock Market

What is the stock market? Wikipedia defines the *stock market* as a market or equity market which is a public entity. Now you may be thinking, what is stock or what are stocks? Not to introduce some business jargons again, just know that stocks are that entity that shows that you own a company or part of a company. The stock market is the biggest market in the world. As an investor or potential investor, you'll need to understand some popular topics which would help you in your investing career.

First, you must become an avid reader of quality investing news, business news, information and all other news vital to your success as a new stock exchange investor. Yes, you can learn about the stock exchange market you can begin trading stocks and risking your own very cash if you don't have the knowledge. There is a lot to learn, and you can never know it all. The next thing to do is to identify your investing objective. Make sure you have an objective. That investment goal is very important. It shouldn't be vague like: I want to be the richest investor, or I want to make much money from investing. That is vague and unacceptable. You should be specific, and your goals should be SMART. In the space of three years, I want to make $120,000 through passive investment. Are your goals realistic? What happens is that many people who go into stock market investment especially as beginners feel that stock market exchange is a good way to make quick money, so they focus more on the short-term investment. This shouldn't be the case a long term strategy is the better choice when it comes to stock exchange.

Furthermore, you need to determine what kind of investment trader you would choose to be. This book is centered on passive investment. So you'll most likely be a passive investor than someone who scalp shares, buys and hold stocks for a long term or swing trades. You should understand that there are levels to this. The knowledge and the understanding must be solid else you'll lose money.

It wouldn't be too early for us to introduce passive income investing. You can continue to do the same thing and expect a different result. Building that passive income would always remain the best way to free yourself from the shackles of financial bondage. But we should note that sometimes we don't create passive income, we just follow it's flow while some would take much initial effort to start because you would need to purchase some assets. Amidst all these, one thing is sure, when it starts giving you income, it never stops.

Basically, there are two types of income sources: Active or earned income and Passive income which is also known as residual income. We know that active income is basically the money you earn as an employee or self-employed individual. This income is linear in nature, meaning that if you stop working, the income stops also. A major disadvantage about active income is that one has to put in a lot of time and energy to maintain it and as frustrating as it could sound, the time and energy you put into it may not worth it.

Throughout the previous chapter, we have been able to prove that financial success hinges on two things: having enough income to support your desired lifestyle, two, having enough time to do what you want. When you own an active income stream, you exchange time for money. Active income alone is not an effective way to create wealth. What you need is passive income.

This type of income is very important for

financial freedom because it is money earned irrespective of whether you actively work or not. You are literarily making money in your sleep. You work as a wealth creator building a business using income-generating assets. What's an asset? Anything that makes money for you. Yes, we can make money while we sleep; however, passive income is not completely hands off.

There are several passive income opportunities like:

1. Real estate (rental income)

2. Franchising

3. Royalties (from books or music)

4. Licensing fees (from products created by you)

5. Affiliate marketing

6. Online advertising revenue

7. Business revenue from selling your

own products and services.

Thank God for property and internet business models. Everything listed above can be executed rightly without much learning. Our generation today has made multiple income streams doable for everybody. This process is a tested and trusted one.

Come to think of it. We really don't have any suggestion on how to create that passive income. But you can take the following steps;

✓ You can start a blog

✓ Create an online course

✓ Build an app

✓ Write an eBook

✓ Create a website and sell products

✓ Rent out your tools

The suggestion could go on and on. It all

depends on the method you want to employ. I would list a few methods here.

First, don't be a landlord; be an investor. A landlord would sit on the income he is receiving from renting just one apartment. An investor would think of more than just one apartment. He/she would invest in more than one business enterprise.

Don't build an active income for your passive funds. Confused? Let me explain this. You are receiving $1500 a month from your housing investment. What is expected of you is to put that money to work, not keep it in the bank to accrue minute interest?

Furthermore, you are going to be learning practical methods from me on how to tap into the provision of passive income to become financially free.

1. Save Like Nobody Owes You Anything. Right from the beginning

of this book, we have stated the importance of savings. It should be noted that when your money starts working for you, you shouldn't spend it all. Invest in other business and save a lot. If you fail to build your overall "Money strength" through the use of some special financial nut, you may fall back to where you started. However, it is important that the savings I am referring to are After-tax savings. What you need to do is save money after contributing your 401K (retirement savings plan sponsored by an employer) and IRAs since you can't safelytouch funds in the pre-tax retirement's accounts until you're 59.5. What I did was that I saved 50-70% of my tax, after 401K contribution every year for 13 years because I was speculating that I wouldn't last for 20 years with my finance. Now, I save 100% of my passive income

2. Find something you love doing and make it a source of income. I love writing and investing. That is why you have this book in your hands. I combined these two interest with my ability to get things done. What did I get? Multiple investment opportunities. Every individual has that field of strength. A place that is very comfortable for them, it could be playing a sport, doing a kind of work, etc. You just need to open your mind to the opportunities around

3. Treat Passive Income Like A Game. Remember the previous chapter; an active income could serve as the beginning step for the passive

income. The initial funding has to come from somewhere. So this is what I mean when I say you should treat it as a game. Don't rush; take it as a journey with different levels. Just like playing a game. If you fail in level one, it is not the end of the game as you have an active income and you can restart.

4. Determine What Income Level Will Make You Happy. This leads us back to our initial goal. You break down your goals into smaller bits. You must have made this decision even before you go into the venture which would provide the passive income.

5. Don't force yourself to start. When you force yourself, things won't work out naturally.

For some, financial freedom has a good

job that pays well every month. And having much excess which they can use to buy fancy cars, a bigger house, or nice vacations. Being able to pay off debt, having a healthy emergency fund and money in the bank account to fund their kid's college. While others believe that financial freedom is number one. They look to sock away a nest egg of $3 million, $4 million, or whatever their number might be. It all begins with you. Make use of the principles in this book. And the sky would just be a starting point.

Passive Index Investment

Passive income is the easiest type of investment. Anyone can literally retire a millionaire with this right strategy making use of passive index investment. However, you should learn to take some hours to pick the winners in this field and follow their footsteps. The simplest and easiest way to make money is by tracking the market. Tracking has to do with monitoring the market. First, we really need to understand what index funds are and how we can start investing as a beginner.

Index funds are now becoming a major force in the investing world. Research has been able to show us that in 2016, more than $1 out of every $5 invested in the stock exchange market was conducted using the index fund. As a new investor is this your concern? Yes. It is because you would need to understand what index funds are, the weaknesses and it's advantages because you must be ready to face all these questions and give a good response because this is the foundation of this book and given that you are a smaller investor you should give index funds a proper look. Briefly, I would talk about index funds; the good, the bad and the horrible. Knowing this would extend your horoscope.

First, what are index funds? To understand what index funds is you should view it from an academic aspect. Basically, it has to do with a person or a committee of people sitting down and coming up with that list of rules of how to build or create a portfolio of individual holdings because when it all comes to that end, the only thing left that you can actually invest in is the single common stocks or bonds. Are you confused? Are you confused? I hope not. Let me give you the example of the most famous index of all time; the Dow Jones Industrial Average which is a list of thirty *blue-chip stocks.* This list is created by the representative collection of stocks which are pivotal to the economy of the U.S. These shares are weighted next based on stock price and adjustments also. Therefore making way for things such as *stock splits.*Stocks like these are selected by the editors of the standard *Wall Street Journal*

& P 500 and even other indices have been overtaken by the Dow Jones Industrial Average. Even over longer periods of time by a meaningful margin based on compounded functions even though the year-to-year results deviates and seems to appear small. We made mention of the S&P f500 which is now the most widely discussed index in the world. The S&P 500 stands for Standard and Poor's 500. It was called the composite index in 1932, but it then expanded to 90 stocks three years later before counting up to 500 in 1957. The S&P 500 has that complex methodology than the Dow Jones Industrial Average. However, inthe past decade, the S&P 500's methodology has changed drastically. The inexperienced investors may find it hard to understand because it is not like the way it used to be in the past. Don't be tired; all these jargons and terminologies would lead to something meaningful.

Investors today are mostly clueless. They really don't know what they are going into. That is why it is very important that you know what you are going into or else you would enter a ship of Theseus paradox and you would wonder what point you are going to face because you can't wrap your head around what is happening.

You should just have it at the back of your mind that an index fund is simply a *mutual fund*. Instead of you to have that portfolio manager making a choice for you, outsourcing that capital allocation job to that individual or committee would determine the index methodology. The Jones Industrial Average index fund or ETF (exchange traded fund) is a mutual fund which trades like that share of stock throughout the day rather than settling at the end of the day like that ordinary fund. Most times it is the same portfolio and even the same underlying holdings. What you are just doing in simple terms is that you're handing over the job of managing your money to professional editors of *The Wall Street Journal.* When you buy an S&P 500 index fund, you're just giving the job of handling your money to a handful of people at Standard and Poors. At the long run, it would end in your own portfolio as your individual stock, or it would just be held in a pooled structure with a portfolio manager over it who is responsible for getting the result as close to the index as possible *this is known as tracking.*

Psychology Of Investment

We are aware that the study of economics and finance is traditionally the assumption that people always behave rationally. However, it is not the case in reality. People behave irrationally. Yes, take that from me. They act or do things which are not of their best interest. The behavioral finance is that combination of psychology and the financial theory also. This is now becoming an academic discipline, and there are several articles which talk about this online. However, they all fail to understand that people make mistakes and those mistakes aren't mistakes they are just wrong decisions for that particular time.

Furthermore, emotional factors such as fear, uncertainty, personal bias, regret aversion, and ego can play so much importance in the life of an investor. Despite efforts to be sensible in monetary matters, we still fall into the same problem and mistakes because of these psychological factors. Experts say that there are cognitive principles which affect our decision making when it comes to money matters. Psychological issues like regret aversion, ego, and personal bias affect the stock market and investment like any other factor. In this chapter, I have been able to draw raw data from these attitudes.

Having said that, one of the most important psychological issues I feel should be treated first is the issue of consistency. When the market falls, do you fold? What happens when issues are not going as planned. What do you do? You have to understand the mindset of an investor to be able to know how investment really works. You can have the mind of an investor, and you wouldn't have any investment. There are several people who just place money into what they feel *would work* and it would happen that they would get enough money in several folds. But the regret aversion is also a strong psychological issue. We hate losing and it takes an asymmetrical attitude to risk it all. When you are faced with losses what do you do? Do you prepare to admit that we have made a mistake or do we begin to assume that losing make us better investors?In the same manner, when we experience gains what do we do? We have that strong attitude, and we boast of how things worked our way right? Common sense should tell us that winners sell to the losers. Sometimes it is senseless to hang on to a stock when it is not doing well right? Well, it is good to be senseless at times. If you so much believe in that stock, you should not be tempted to double up on it.

More also, the rule of thumb and overconfidence are also two psychological products which affect an investor. Some investors, including professionals, tend to be overly confident in their ability to make the right decision. Well, it extends from many things we do in our everyday life. Investors seem to be clearly overconfident of their abilities and accuracy of their predictions. Making an investment is not a bet. It is okay to be prudent and objective in manner. You should learn how to make mistakes and improve. The rule of thumb is also a psychological factor which affects the investor. The rule of thumb requires an investor to hold a stock that has done well before but id doing badly now, thinking that it would go back to how it was before.

Lastly, the house money effect. Okay, things are going well; your investment is yielding so much. Then you feel like, *why can't I add more, I should make it bigger than before.* If an investor has that good run with some investments, he/she is tempted to take one higher level of risk with future investment. Well, the truth remains that not all similar principles have similar solutions. There are a few strange cases.

How To Purchase Index Funds

Warren Buffet, the greatest investor in the history of the stock market and even one of the richest people in the history of America, is attributed to a saying that *investors should know their limitations*. Well, those words are very simple and easy to understand and apply in everyday life. However, you should know what you are capable of doing and what you can't do. Ask yourself if you got a chance to fight with that grizzly bear. You say that this is crazy because the bear is big and it would probably kill you but do you get that picture? Are you doing more than you can? Are you biting off more than you can chew? There are a lot of people on Wall Street that are successful. Those who fight bears and bulls every day and they overcome. Oh, yes, I know. This chapter is not about bears and bulls. But if you are thinking of purchasing an index fund, you should be ready to become the bear or the bull. As a new investor, nothing beats index funds because they are simple and secure ways to invest and prosper in the stock market. Index funds allow investors to relax. Is it a secure way to allow some individuals to take your burdens right? Whether investing on your own or taking advantage of index funds, you should know your limitations.

The index mutual funds are laisezz-fair, easy, low-cost and cover a large horoscope of stock investment. There are three simple steps to follow if you want to purchase index funds.

- Decide where to buy
- Pick an index
- Check investment minimum and another cost.

Chose where to buy the index fund. You chose to purchase that index fund directly from a mutual fund company or a brokerage any decision you make is fine. Same goes for the exchange-traded funds now. Let us hit the nail on the head. *Fund selection.* Is the first thing that should be Where do you want to buy them? From various fund families? From the big mutual fund companies? You must carry out that selection, and you must not limit everything to what is available or a discount broker's lineup. Furthermore, you should also consider convenience. Looking for a single provider who is ready to accommodate all your needs, for example, is very important to make sure that your mutual funds become okay. If you're just going to invest in a mutual fund or you are going for a mix of funds you should find a mutual fund company able to serve you that investment hub.

But if you need such sophistication in your stock research, you need to go out and do that yourself. Pick that research and screening tool, that discount broker who sells index funds. You may even need to open a brokerage account. When picking where to buy you should remember that there is also commission-free options. There are kinds of options do not offer transaction-fee mutual funds or commission-free ETFs. Don't forget that selecting or picking discount brokers would definitely affect the success of your investment. The selection should be from Charles Schwab, E-Trade, Fidelity and TD Ameritrade. They are all worth checking out. Lastly, the trading cost should also be another factor that you should consider when deciding to buy funds. If the commission or transaction of the fee isn't waived, think of how much a broker or fund company would charge you to buy or sell the index fund. These mutual fund commissions are higher than the stock trading ones. Some would be $20.

Picking an index. The index of mutual funds would track various indexes. The Standard & Poor's 500 index is one of the best-known indexes because it has that permanent 500 companies it tracks which includes several large, and well known U.S- based businesses. I don't think I have been able to see an index having more than that. But we should know that the S&P 500 is not the only index in town. There are several other indexes which are based on the composition of stock and other assets also like the company size and capitalization, geography, business sector or industry, asset types, and even the market opportunities.

Even though there are arrays of choices, you should need to know the one that would be perfect for you. Warren Buffet did say that the average investor needs only invest in a broad stock market index to be properly diversified.

Checking investment minimum and the other cost is also very important. The low cost is one of the biggest selling points of index funds. Because the truth is that nobody wants to spend much to make much. Well, that is the truth. The investments are easy and cheap to run because they have that automated structure. It follows with the shifts in value in an index. However, you shouldn't assume that all value in an index are cheap or cost low. Sometimes, they may not be actively managed by a team of a well-paid analyst but still, carry administrative costs. This cost would be subtracted from each fund shareholder's returns as that percentage of the overall investment. You should consider the following during the checking investment process:

- Investment minimum: The smallest fund required to invest could go as low as a few thousand ($2000). However, once you've been able to cross that threshold, most investors would definitely want to add more money in smaller increments.

- Account minimum: The brokerage's account minimum is $0, and it is common for customers who open a traditional or Roth (IRA). But you should understand that there is a big difference between investment minimum and account minimum.

- Expense ratio. It is one of the main cost which is subtracted from each fund a shareholder returns as the percent of the overall investment. You can find the expense ratio in that mutual fund prospectus or when you call up a quote of a mutual fund on any financial site. The annual expense ratio was 09% for the stock index funds and 0.07% for the bond index funds. Furthermore, you should understand the tax-cost ratio which is in addition to paying fees, owning the fund could also trigger capital gain taxes if it is held outside tax-advantaged accounts like a 401(k) or the IRA.

Portfolio Ideas

In this chapter, you would be exposed to different kinds of portfolio ideas. It is not really an idea but a standardized process. However, we can't possibly go into the portfolio ideas without talking about the portfolio types. There are different types of portfolio types, I wouldn't go into all, but I would only talk about those that concern us as index investors.

The first portfolio that should be on this list is the aggressive portfolio. As the name sounds; It is aggressive. You'll be facing stocks that are high in risk and also high reward also — coupled with that fact that the stocks in this category would either help you have that high beta, or it would reduce it. Stocks which have high beta continually experience fluctuations. This means that they are not stable and their instability has so much to do with the overall market.Individuals having aggressive stock offerings in the early stages of growth always have that unique value proposition. If you intend to build that portfolio you should look for common household names, check online for companies which are rapidly accelerating earnings. This would require you to scrutinize that technology but many firms in other sectors would be pursuing that same thing as well.

Furthermore, the defensive portfolio is also another type of portfolio. This is when you put defensive stocks in your harem. What this suggests is that you don't have a high beta stock in your portfolio. These kind of stocks are not prone to instability. The income portfolio is also another kind of portfolio. But this one deals with making money from the dividends and other types of stakeholders and distributors. This looks like the defensive stocks, but instead of having a lower income, it would offer you higher yields. Furthermore, the income portfolio brings positive cash flow as well as the Real Estate Invest Trust (REITs). MLP (Master Limited Partnership) and many more are excellent avenues for getting those income-producing investment.

If you are looking for an investment that is the closest thing to pure gamble, you have a speculative portfolio. Just as it sounds, it is speculative, rough, tentative. And since it is just like a gamble, you have more risk involved than any other portfolio discussed here. The investor gurus have suggested that out of one's investable assets, 10% falls under the speculative. You might want to be of the opinion that the widespread of Leverage ETFs in the recent market happens because of the high increase in the speculative portfolios. This may be true, but we should not forget that this kind of portfolio requires so much attention and carefulness, therefore, picking the right investment would require a special kind of skill something I believe most people don't have. Speculative stocks require so much study and attention to every detail.

You might be thinking of shaping your portfolio to the hybrid level. The hybrid is the combination of several investments like bonds, commodities, real estate, art, just anything you can think of that can fetch you money in the long run. Following the regular principle of investment, this type of portfolio would entail blue-chip stocks and even have some high-grade government corporate bonds entrenched in it. REITs and MLP's would not be left out too. Fundamentally, what a hybrid portfolio would have is that beautiful and low-risk mix of different stocks and bonds in different sizes and proportions, but all remained fixed. Since you're dipping your hands into several investments and blending them perfectly, you are actively involved in diversification. Furthermore, an approach like this would give so many benefits due to the equities and the fixed income securities.

For the indexfunds portfolios, there are three simple portfolio strategies. First is the *two fund portfolio* which includes two major funds; the global stock market fund and the U.S investment grade bond. Both are vanguard funds which blend into the total Bond Market ETF (Ticker: BND), and this holds the mortgage securities also.

We shouldn't forget our lazy people. That is why we have a lazy portfolio. It is good to be lazy. Laziness brings out that creativity and it would make you complete a job of two weeks in two days because of too much procrastination on your part. This portfolio is divided into two; the U.S only fund and the international fund also. Making use of this strategy, an individual would be able to regulate the amount of U.S dollar investments. The dollar is a global currency. I am sure you know that right?

The last is *The core 4 Portfolio*. This kind or type of portfolio is carved out of the U.S commercial real estate and has a separate class. The commercial real estate's makes up about 13 percent of the U.S. economy and yet represents only 3 percent of the stock market, maybe because the stock market has the highest number of gurus. And another reason why I think this happens is that most commercial real estate is privately owned rather than that scrutinized tradable investment from the government.

Basics Of FIRE

Fire? Let's get the extinguisher. FIRE (Financial Independence and early retirement). That sound better right? Well, for now, Fire is having that moment. It is not hard to understand, and it is not hard to appeal. Financial independence sounds cool. There is nothing as good as being your own boss. You'll be able to go on vacation and do what you like. The Fire movement is something that quickly gains momentum. Now, you're thinking, what is Fire exactly?

Well, when you are thinking of your retirement age, you probably think that it would be in the '50s or '60s. Well, that is good. However it is the norm, and the social security administration would only allow you to start taking benefits at age 62. Take for example you can start to get your funds from your retirement account without penalty at age 59 ½ .

Even though we are aware of that retirement age, it is advisable for us to start FIRE very early especially when we are in our 30's or 40's. Some even start in their 20's. Early retirement is the major aim of FIRE, but there is more to it than that.

Financial independence ultimately means that you can shape your life without taking money into consideration, most of us have to consider our finances in nearly every decision we make, or maybe even make decision solely based on money. But once we reach financial independence, we get the freedom not to be bossed around by what we earn or what we have saved. A good reason to retire early is that you have an alternate vision for your life that you are eager to pursue, but which you can't pursue while employed full time, Achieving financial independence allowed us to leave that career chapter of our lives from a place of gratitude and appreciation, and move onto our next chapter that we're in control of

    - Tanja Hester, a recent FIRE graduate and founder of the website *Our Next Life.*

I am sure you're still wondering what really is this Fire? It is a movement which follows one simple rule; *spend less than you earn and save difference in low-fee investments like index funds*- Hester.

The beauty about Fire is that it is a retirement plan which wants you to retire early.

"Retiring early because you don't like your job is a bad reason to do it and is a recipe for being bored or aimless when you get there," she said. "Achieving FIRE is a big deal, and it takes a lot of focus and determination. It's not for those who want to get rich quick, or for those who just hate their job. The better solution then is just to

find a new job or a new career path. I'm a huge believer that you can love your job and still want to retire early or just achieve financial independence! That was true for us. We loved our work, the people we worked with, and our clients, but we didn't love the pace of it, the pressure or the constant travel."

Hayes, another graduate of FIRE

We shouldn't forget that other sources of income are important parts of these financial freedom process. Because the less money you need to live, the less money you need to save in order to fund the rest of your years. Let us do the math:

To highlight the value of cutting expenses, for every $100 per month you can trim, it means you need $30,000 less to achieve FI ($1,200 yearly expense x 25 = $30,000).

The three basic elements to FIRE are; time, expenses and income. However, the goal is to put that space between the expenses and the income making sure that you spend little while you gain more. The rules are quite easy, and you'll definitely want to jump on it but getting there, attaining that level can be a problem if you are not ready to leave that disciplined life. The only way to have that strong determination is to have a *strong why*. Hayes did say. *"If you want to retire early, you need to have a strong 'why Do you want to quit your job so that you can start that business you always talked about with your friends? Do you want to have more than two weeks per year of vacation time? Do you want to spend more time with your loved ones? Whatever you're why to let that be the motivating factor to create a plan and stick to it during the tough times. Once you have that why you want to determine your path."*

You should be very specific about what you want and how you're going to get there. The truth is that this book, all of it centers on the most fundamental principles which you know, and you've been listening to since childhood. SAVINGS.

Do not save what is left after spending, but spend what is left after saving – Warren Buffet

Power Of Compound Interest

"The most powerful force in the universe is compound interest."

-

Albert

Einstein

That quote shouldn't be from a science prodigy, guru and legend. What does he know about compound interest? Well, investment, a stock market, and stock exchange are simple math and probability. That is not my concern though.

Ask any individual about compound interest and you'll hear him/her say; *yeah, I know it. I know little or something about it.* Well, if you truly understand compound interest, you wouldn't be where you are now. You wouldn't have so much bad credit and a lot of debts from credit cards. The sad truth is that the financial sector makes use of the general public. They want to make millions from you while you suffer to make ends meet.

Compound interest to me should first be explained mathematically. It is interest that is paid on interest and principal over a long period of time. Let's say you have some $10,000 today and you make 3% each year from your bank. You would have $10,300 by the end of the year. If you leave it there for the second year, you would have $10,609 the third year would be $10,927. This is so small, isn't it? But when compound interest comes in you'll have compounded a 10% per year deal and you'll have doubled the money in 7 years. In 28 years you would have about $160,000. $160,000 from $10,000 within two decades and eight years doing nothing. Do you get that?

However, we shouldn't cover our eyes to the fact that credit card charges would work against us and our bank is only teaching us to calculate the interest daily which is *supposed* to be to our advantage. You see that they make use of your money to get more money while they hand over peanuts to you. Well, mutual funds and stocks, typically only provide yearly dividends. Likewise, the banks on their fixed deposit are yearly also. Very pathetic interest rates. Compounding is a very good way to get the best from your residual funds. Especially funds that you don't intend to spend anytime soon. For compound interest to work, you would need to set that compounding frequency. The more frequent it happens, the better it is. You can start to compound your funds quarterly. Compounding by seconds is ideal, and it is one of the best ways to enjoy compounding, it is better than yearly compounding. Using this incredible force would help you to break the chains of financial restraints. Furthermore, if you want to choose an investment vehicle for compounding, you should make sure that;

- It has excellent returns (minimum of 5%)
- It has frequent compounding (at least monthly)
- Low risk with a high winning percentage is involved. At least 90%
- It allows you to withdraw whatever you want, whenever you want. You can decide to stop anytime you wish.

I keep telling people about taking that particular step as soon as they find it convincing. I would also tell you the same here. Before Bitcoin became what it is today. I remember that there was a time that 1BTC was $105. I wanted to buy it,but I was so skeptical. I feared that it would crash and something might just happen. I pushed it aside and faced other investment opportunities. Fast forward to November 2017, BTC is $10,000. Okay, I knew I had missed the opportunity, but I was so sure that it was going to go down once more. And it was down again. Whatever step you want to take, take it now. You shouldn't sleep on it. Nobody find's a treasure or money buried beneath, wouldn't you dig to find it?

Ever since the 1970's the United States dollars has been following that consistent trend of 5-7 years of cycles of up and down trends. This is not the late 2001 or 2002 leave the money over there then forget about it for a while. That is savings in the simple comment all; it shows that you're the only one thinks about transportation when we are talking about the life and death of a patient.

Starting people is always happy because he walks in and makes a sum grow faster than it was before because she did earpiece, there was an attritionist (Someone would add or place something there.) so the question on your lips. Fist, do you really make $250? Well, definitely been helping her for a while now. Do you know that age 25 group, you'll accumulate $878,570 by age 65? The shorter the wire, the more efficient it is. You should get your body ready for the simplest investment process. As an employee, being faithful to the initial instructions from the doctor but you later fail to understand or follow the rest because you feel that you don't need to.

Selecting Your Asset Allocation

Is Life about balance and choice right? Our investing lives are divided into two broad stages making use of just two funds: *the wealth Acquisition stage* and the *Wealth Preservation stage.* But you can simply blend both right?

VTSAX (Vanguard Total Stock Market Index Fund) and VBTLX (Vanguard Total Bond Market Index Fund) are two broad aspects of the indexing funds.

When you are investing with the mentality of wealth acquisition, you are working to gain more money, save and invest again. VTSAX is the most preferred here. Financial independence must be your goal so your savings rate must be high and right also. As you invest that money each month, you allow the market's wild ride go smooth. Then you get into the world of wealth preservations. This is when you decide to step away from your job and the regular paychecks you receive, and you begin to live on only your income from investment. Sounds risky? Yes, because you wouldn't have any extra fund to fall but to incase *something happens*, however, adding bonds to the portfolio like the fresh cash you'll be investing would help your bonds have that smooth investment ride. In the real world, you might not be able to make the distinction between making some money in retirement and out of retirement because investment shouldn't be about retirement. Remember FIRE right?

However, to create this solid framework of asset allocation, we should know that these two additional factors would provide you with that balance you need.

First, you'll need effort. There was a study which shows that allocation provides the best return over time but it is not the same at all and this suggests that adding a smaller percentage of bonds like 10-20% would outperform the 100% stocks. But you should note that the 100% is an 80/20% mix. How these results would unfold over the years is something that is unpredictable, and for this reason, we should learn to favor simplicity. Having said that if you're willing to put more effort or work hard you can see slightly smooth out the wild ride and you can possibly outperform them over time by adding the 10-25% bonds. If you take this step for once in a year, you would be able to rebalance your funds and to maintain your chosen allocation also. You might also want to rebalance your funds anytime the market makes that major move (20% +) up or down. This would require you to either sell shares in whichever asset class that has performed better or to buy shares in the one lagging.

We all know that basically, what bonds do is to smooth the ride and stocks power the returns. However, the more you hold in stocks, the better your results and the more gut-wrenching volatility you'll need to endure and finally scale through. If you're thinking of holding a stock, you must not think, but you must be mentally tough enough to do this so that you'll not panic when they plunge. And you should not make the mistake that you would own them forever, they would surely plunge, and they would plunge at the most unexpected times.

The Market Must Crash!

Yes, you read that right. The market must crash; in fact, it should crash. In fact, market crashes are to be expected. You are new to what happened in 2008. It had happened before, and it would happen again and again. I have been in the investing game for almost 40 years now, and in that time we've had

- ✓ The great recession of 1974-1975. Some of you wouldn't know this because you're new investors.
- ✓ The massive inflation of the late 1970s & early 1980 also. WIN (Whip Inflation Now). This was when mortgages rates were pushing 20%, and you could buy 10-year treasuries paying just 15%+
- ✓ The infamous 1989 Business week cover which read: *The Death Of Equities*. The death gave rise to the

greatest comeback bull market of all time. This didn't stop the crash of

✓ 1987. This is one of the Biggest one day drop in history. Many brokers were literally on the window ledges, and even some took that leap.

✓ What followed next is the recession of the early '90s.

✓ Then the Tech rash of the late '90s

✓ Followed by the deadly 9/11

✓ Then there was a little dust-up in 2008.

Somehow, the market would always recover. And if someday it really doesn't then there is no investment that would be safe, and none of this financial knowledge and strategies would matter anyway. Looking at the bright side of things, the S&P 500 that broader and more telling index grew at an annualized rate of 11.9%. This means amidst all these, if you had invested $1,000 then you would probably have $89,790 as 2015 dawns that is one of the many impressive results from these disasters. What you need to do is *toughen up and let it ride*. You should allow that to sink. The stock market and investment are not for the weak. The market would always go up; you should understand that it wouldn't always be a smooth ride. How you take control of that ridiculous increase would determine how you would handle the depressing days also. Take a moment to look at the chart of the stock market over time look at the trend and relentless disaster after and even the disaster up. Notice something? The truth is that the next 10, 20, 30 or 40 years would have so much collapse, recession, and even disasters also. When this is about to happen or when it is happening, you should toughen up and learn to ignore the noise while you stay the course and ride out of the storm.

Funny enough, you should know that bad things are coming, and you should expect them.

Best Index Funds For The Long Term

The best index funds always have low expenses and diversified portfolios which can definitely stand the test of time. But it should be noted that not all index funds are diversified and some are not proper for long-term investment. There is a wide variety of index funds to choose from, and because of this, it is important that an investor should understand the best needs an index fund attracts.

The S&P 500 Index fund is the most popular kind of index fund, but there are different kinds also. First, we have the Vanguard 500 Index (VFINX). This is a mutual fund that is available for the public, and it became active through the mind-blowing business idea of Vanguard investments, Jack Bogle who did study market and also took note that most traders don't beat the average market levels and they have been able to factor the expenses. Therefore, if by simply buying that low-cost mutual fund which is the basket of stocks found in the index then the investors would be able to capture reasonable returns also. The VFINX has that expense ratio of just 0.16 percent, and the minimum initial investment is $3,000.

The next is the Fidelity Spartan 500 index (FUSEX). Because of its size, fidelity made sure that its indexing comes close to that of Vanguard and it is always second to that of vanguard as it offers the expense ratio of just 0.10 percent with the minimum initial investment which could be as low as $2,500. FUSEX holds the same stocks as VFINX, but the expense ratio is quite low.

Schwab S&P 500 Index is the next best index for the long term purpose. For Charles Schwab, he has been able to make that conscious effort to provide more than just discount brokerage services to investors, but he has been able to dig deep into the index funds markets of Vanguard and Fidelity to bring out something good. In recent years, the discount broker has been able to lower the expenses just to compete for head to head with Vanguard and Fidelity. The expense ratio is as low as 0.09 percent, and the minimum initial investment is a ridiculous $100.

This chapter will be incomplete if we fail to mention the best aggressive stock index funds. As a long-term investor, you wouldn't mind seeing market fluctuations and your account balance just going up and down in a very short period right? So, you'll find aggressive stock index funds very attractive.

Vanguard Growth Index (VIGRX) is the first on this list. This fund invests only in the large cap stocks which have growth potential. Although it is a bit risky, it has much potential rewards and winnings in the long run than even the S&P 500 index funds. The expense ratio is 0.22%, and the minimum initial investment is $3,000.

Fidelity NASDAQ Composite Index (FNCMX). This index like the Vanguard growth consists of fat, large-cap stocks which would give you a greater long-term growth potential than the broad market indices. If the added risk is okay for this long-term return potential, you'll be attracted to the FNCMX which has a ratio of 0.29 percent and a minimum initial investment of $2500.

For the best Bond Index Funds, there are two major options which fall under the bracket of index funds we've been using for a while now. The Vanguard Total Bond Market Index (VBMFX) and the Fidelity Total Bond (FTBFX) also. The Vanguard has an expense ratio of 0.16 percent, and that minimum initial investment is $3,000 while that of fidelity is a 0.45 percent expense ratio and a $2500 minimum initial purchase.

Financial Freedom

Have you ever felt trapped in a Rat Race and wished you could retire quickly with enough money in your bank account? You must have felt that you are spending way too much than you are earning, right?

Have you ever felt that you are only helping your boss to get the life that you want or deserve? Have you ever felt that you are spending most of your life building the dreams of others and not yours? Well, that feeling is mutual. Sometimes in the past, I felt frustrated because I was deep in debt, I thought I wouldn't be able to retire because I felt that as soon as I do so, the money will stop coming and thus I wouldn't be able to pay off my mortgages and credit card. We feel trapped because there are too many bills to pay, too many dreams to fulfill and it seems as if we have little or no time. Take a few moments to think of the reason why you work. If your answer is to make money, then I am afraid that you are still caught up in that rat race. Most individuals would tie themselves to the shackles of their job and debt because they feel there is no way of escape.

You have a choice!

You have that liberty to decide when you want to work, without thinking of your boss or thinking that your career is at stake. In fact, you'll have that freedom to go on that vacation you so much desire troubles of retrenchments thereafter. There is nothing as good as freedom. I can tell you that. I am sure you really crave for financial freedom, if not you wouldn't be reading this book right now. How do you think you can be free financially? Are you getting a better job with a higher paycheck? I am sorry to disappoint you, but that wouldn't work. When you have high paychecks you would be thinking of an expensive lifestyle right, and even more, responsibilities would begin to come your way, then you begin to work more hours. It all leads back to the same circle.

If you can get a good grip on this, you would be exposed to the fact that financial freedom is not measured by how long you are working. You don't work hard. You work smart. Consequently, financial freedom is definitely not about amazing abundant riches or getting that golden lifestyle.

Now, you may think that there is nothing like financial freedom. And craving for financial freedom isn't realistic. Well, that's just your feelings. Financial freedom is possible. It is important for you to know now that ordinary people have achieved financial freedom if you think you have to be as rich as Bill Gates, Jeff Bezos, Jack Ma or Oprah Winfrey before you achieve it, you are probably having the wrong line of thought.

Before we think of financial freedom, first is financial freedom a reality?

As I have mentioned earlier, if you think financial freedom is unrealistic, please save yourself the time and effort by dropping this book. But if you want to achieve financial freedom and you believe that it is possible to be free from the rat race, then immerse all the contents in this book and make sure you practice them. Financial freedom is not an impossible fantasy.

All of us dream of financial freedom; however many of us think that it is just something in the abstract or some kind of fantasy. Most times we think about it from time to time, sigh and forget it. We do this because we have that believe that a state as good as financial freedom is only reserved for millionaires in the world. Can this freedom ever be a reality? Even when we accept that it is a reality, we think it only applies to the super-rich.

Nonetheless, the truth remains that financial freedom cannot be possible with this kind of mental attitude. If you want to be financially free, you have to believe that it is possible to be financially free. Next, you need to build your confidence. You have to be confident that anyone, yes, anyone can be financially free, provided that he/she is willing to work towards it. If you fail to have this positive attitude, you are never going to make it. So the very first step would be to fine-tune your mentality and believe in it from your inside. You can design your life the way you prefer it all depends on you. Now you may be thinking; *why is he telling me to believe in something I know little or nothing about.* The truth remains that if you take this book and read it passively if you fail to put the information into use, you probably didn't believe in financial freedom. You may decide that you may want to gain financial freedom by starting your own business. What should you do? Have a vision for it. Think of a business that no one has thought of before. Is this possible? Yes, it is. And it starts by believing in yourself, trusting yourself that you can do it. Even if your idea exists, you should execute it differently. Execution is what makes you different from your competitors. There is no point in starting something for financial security and having no faith in it. If you do not earn enough money to support your dream of being a financially free person, then you need to find means of making money to make such dreams come true.

I would try to make this as quickly as possible — a short story of how I became financially independent in 5 years. Note; I am not a very close relative of Gate's or brother to Mark. I am as ordinary as you could think I am. However, this isn't a formula. So don't think you have to follow the details of what I did to reach a similar goal. When I began my journey towards financial freedom, I didn't consider it as a journey to financial freedom. I just had that goal that I wanted to do things differently, and I wanted to go faster — 3-4 years instead of 5. I wanted to make a six-figure income. The truth remains that as we gain in knowledge and wisdom, our priorities change from what seems to be less important to bigger perspectives having pivotal goals. First of all, we need to get some things straight about me. I have never been dumb with money. I have never been in the red zone. And please note that I am not saying this to feel good about myself. But just to let you know that most times, you are born with some innate qualities which give you "an upper hand" over others. At a point in my life, I realized that my expensive hobbies had to go and be replaced with "free" hobbies. Most times, I would save to buy a computer, then an SLR camera, then a HiFi rack then I would save to get another computer, then a telescope. It took me time to make the connection between hobbies and things that can get me money.

Somehow, I got influenced by two personal finance books; one of which we all know *Rich Dad Poor Dad* and *Your money or your life*. I learned how to calculate my real wage by subtracting taxes, transport, business clothes, cost of living, etc. from the later. The Rich Dad

Poor Dad standard made me think like a poor person and save and pay in cash. I was probably on the way to think like a middle-class person who buys everything on credit. What weighs down the middle class is a large set of liabilities in the form of house payments, car payments, credit payments, educational payments, etc. Having these liabilities make it hard for you to replace them with assets.

At first, I started by just putting my money in savings accounts and watch them grow. But what seems to be very key here is that I did not start investing for the first 3 years out of the 6 years it took me to gain financial freedom. Another thing I noticed early is those small expenditures added up quickly. $10 there, $100 there, $50 there, $5 every day for the month and you wouldn't know when you have little or nothing to save. In months were I bought very little my savings seemed to go up very fast. I tapped into the provision of opportunity cost. I found out that you don't need to spend a lot of money to be *comfortable.*

Furthermore, I made my lifestyle as simple as possible. I relied more on skills and adaptation to the environment rather than thinking of money. As funny as it sounds, I began looking for substitutes for shampoo or toothpaste. I even knew how to make baking soda! I could cook with almost no heat and very few utensils. What was I driving at? Budgeting, budgeting, and budgeting. I had to cut the cost of living drastically. Apart from budgeting, I wanted to make everything I truly needed to live well fit into a couple of large suitcases and reduce my expenditures to what is considered somewhat below the poverty level while I maintained a comfortable lifestyle.

When I got my Ph.D., I had no student debt. I became an academic researcher, and I was about making as much as a state trooper or a long haul trucker. I still searched for creative ways to save money. More also having just graduated with a Ph.D. and paired everything I could possibly need into a couple of large suitcases. I moved to my new job with everything in a couple of suitcases. Before my arrival, I had decided that after 4 years of sharing a kitchen and bathroom with over 15 other people, I wanted the luxury of my own kitchen and my own bathroom. I was so lucky to find a room on top of a house which the Landlord rented to students and researchers. It was within walking distance of my new job, so I was good to go. The only problem I had was how to move my bank accounts. So after a week of eating out with my new boss, etc. I was down to a couple of cans of tuna, a large bag of rice, and some soy sauce for the second week until I got my paycheck.

Because I was able to cut all my expenses to the bare essentials, I was able to save approximately 60-90% of my net income through grad school and my subsequent jobs with an average percentage in the mid-eighties. At first, this money went directly to my savings account. I fumbled early into investing early. When I say this most people ask about it so here it goes.

At the end of 2005, I was getting tired of earning just 1.5% in my savings accounts. I needed more. Since I grew up in a country where investing in stocks was considered too speculative I started to do my personal research. I called my bank and told them that I wanted to buy some bonds. I have directed to some Baa-rated something bonds. It was a company which finances ships at 3%, and I put down $20,000 at 3%. I was earning $600 a year. I needed something doing so I made a program to predict my net worth. I would type in my assets, and the return on investment (ROI) would appear coupled along with my monthly contribution. This process would calculate my net worth for the next 80 years. I put in statements like "if this" then "this" "if that" then this, "financial independence reached at 4% withdrawal", "my first million," "and my second million" etc. I ran this program twice a day, and I knew my net worth down to the cent. Then I was a young and enthusiastic person, pretty much ignorant about anything investment or business. I was completely clueless. But I remembered that I had much interest in geopolitics and demographic trends. I called my broker once more and told him I wanted to buy some stock in a company producing insulin (because people were getting older and fatter) I also telephoned a telephone company, wind power company, and a small cap holding company. Later I also got an airline company too. You see serious danger right? But as it happened, most positions turned out to perform well except for the airline. I was getting returns of 30% a year. I sold the airline and the wind company too. The funny thing is that today, I wish I had put all my money in those stocks and not just the fraction I did then. (about $40,000). Making these investments drastically increased my ROI. And in my program, I also had an average estimated monthly investment income as well as my average monthly expenses. My investment story turns out to be very complicated by the fact that I was learning more rapidly than the market. Within a year I started pulling money out of the funds to begin a broker account. I read tons of 400 pages of books on how to manipulate the return structure of your investment.

My math geeks may want to consider this. You can skip this paragraph if you find it complex. I am just using this instance, examples, and stories to tell you that being financially free isn't something abstract. Saving 70-80% means spending only 20-30% right? Really small? Well if expenses can be covered by extracting 4% from savings and investments annually, one needs to save a total of 20-30%/0.04=500-750%. Without adding the compound interest etc. this would take 500/80=6.25 years or 750/70=10.7 years. What are the two important conclusions here? One, the 10% difference between 70% and 80% makes a big difference in the estimated time which takes to gain financial freedom. Second, compound interest will only play a minor role. It can move the retirement date to 4 or5 years instead of 6 years. The standard recommended 15% savings rate results in 25 years. This result isn't a coincidence as this is very comparable to the time most people spend working before they retire. Having a long time compound interest doesn't make any difference.

Like you know, things have changed a lot since I started. I recalled celebrating when my first investment went up by $2-"Like a babe, I earned $2 on the stock market today!" but nowadays my portfolio fluctuates sometimes by a paycheck on a daily basis. Gaining or losing our digit figures is not a big deal anymore. "Oh, babe by the way I lost/made $5,000 last week." I still sleep well at night.

How do I look at myself today? "Me, Inc." instead of "Who Cares, Inc." What my day job does is to generate a consistent alpha that is a time-based performance. However, must of my income is beta (market-based). I take control of my own investments, and this has turn into investing into a second job for me. In fact, I can earn more managing my investments than I could, taking on a second (minimum wage) job. This is why I presently, I don't need a "real job."

If I can do this, you can do much more. Financial freedom is not a myth. It has never been, and it could never be. My long and boring story has been able to show you that you need first to believe in yourself, believe in your plan, work out that plan which includes taking action, stay with it, develop yourself and watch how freedom becomes a reality.

I would want you to look at financial freedom has *not having to work anymore in order to live, because your money will be working harder than you do. It will pay your bills, your food, and even your play. The earlier you get there.* Almost everyone wants to be financially free. That definition of financial freedom is very true; in fact, 100% true. However, that's not all about financial freedom. Yes, you have money, "somuch" money that you don't need to work but have you ever felt so empty because you are idle. We crave for financial freedom, but some of us find it hard to stay unoccupied. Financial freedom is managing your time and making the best of it.

In the process of becoming   financially free, there are several stumbling blocks along the way which you have to overcome. These stumbling blocks are called; Financial Hurdle. One of my favorite quotes from Manoj Arora's *From the Rat Race to Financial Freedom* talks about being different and achieving what the extraordinary can only dare to do. *To achieve what 1% of the world's population have (Financial Freedom), you must be willing to do what only 1% dare to do. Hard work and perseverance of highest order.*

This takes us to the first obstacle to financial freedom. YOU! Yes, you. You can be your own stumbling block. *You are only as rich as your willpower-* Wayne Chirisa. Most times we wait when we suppose to move and spend when we are expected to invest. You need to overcome every fear, every unbelief. Personally, you can be an obstacle to yourself if you lack the following things:

- Education: Sadly, your salary has no manual like those appliances you buy. There is no operation manual on how you spend the money you earn. So most times you end up not budgeting or spending more than you can afford and not investing. The soonest you can educate yourself, the better you will be in the position to do something about your financial servitude. Now education is not about going to school. Just because I mentioned obtaining my Ph.D. in the previous chapter doesn't mean that I am *highly* educated. Education is applying that wealth of knowledge acquired by the individual study of a particular subject matter or experiencing life lessons that provide an understanding of something. It is way beyond four walls of a school.

To be able to become financially free, Education is the best defense and Action is the best offense- Dr. Pinky Intal

- Action but have education: Yes, you may know what to do, but you have a fear of taking that leap. Educating yourself without action is meaningless. A total waste of time.

Just as I have mentioned earlier in the book, you should read with an open mind. The next few points I would give now may surprise you. The truth is bittersweet. Take it, think about it and channel your life towards it.

Another personal hurdle may be your parents or close relative. Does it sound surprising? However, not all parents or close relatives are created equal. You should know that some become your ally and support you while others become obstacles of your dream to be financially free. Being a financial consultant for years, I have been able to observe that there are big factors in making financial decisions and the source of these decisions are as important as the decision itself. If you have parents born in the mid-'90s, they are probably not open to things like insurance, investment for retirement, etc. Most people who are not adaptto changing often oppose them. Nevertheless, if you are already at your right age, you have that freedom to make the decision yourself. You combine education with your freedom of choice. With that, you can never go wrong. Matthew B. Brock, CFP says; *Generation Y is constantly being told that there is a right way to plan financially. This advice often comes from an older generation whose financial status doesn't show that their way is the right way.* Being financially free also requires some level of freedom. Mental freedom.

Your spouse could be an obstacle to financial freedom. Actually, what she doesn't know would hurt you. The same applies to you. What you don't know would hurt her. If you spend time investing in yourself, educating yourself financially but your spouse remains ignorant, he/she can put both of you down. Definitely, in every financial decision, it remains important for you to be honest with your spouse. Where the problem lies is when you wanted to act, and she fails to go along with you, the family suffers for it. When seeking advice from financial experts, you don't go alone. Go with your spouse. Make sure both of you are present there so that you can be educated together on the best decision to take for your family.

Let me share a true story here.

Kimberly and Blake are married with 5 children. Blake works as a seaman; Kimberly takes care of their kids. One day, he met Sarah (a financial expert). As a financial expert Sarah suggested, he gets life insurance to be able to establish a good financial foundation first before they even invest. Since he is the only breadwinner and he got lots of dependents. Blake told Kimberly, but Kimberly declines. What she wanted was more savings so that they could go to Manila as vacation and besides, she reasoned that Blake has life insurance coverage as a seaman. The premium on life insurance is like an added expense to her. Then the unexpected happens, while Blake is in the Philippines for vacation, he met a tragic car accident which killed him. The life insurance policy as a seaman is not applicable. Kimberly has to work now to support his 5 children. In the end, the wife's wrong choice took them both away from their children. Blake, dying without leaving anything to their children and Kimberly as a mother now need to work night and day to support her kids. She ended up leaving their children to relatives.

A tragic story right? This happens all the time though. Let me end this point with this: *Wives from time to time object to Life Insurance. . . Widows Never Do!*

The norm of the society can also come as a stumbling block to financial freedom. What do we do now? We buy the latest gadget, travel to different places, have luxurious celebrations, etc. These things aren't bad at all. But when you see your friends having these, the desire to have them for yourself intensifies. Truth be told, lifestyle upgrade isn't a bad idea. But before you think of upgrading your lifestyle make sure you already have the proper financial foundation in place. Make sure you have it laid down for you. The basic needs for you and your family should be present. You should be sure that you have gotten yourself out of every debt, you have saved up for emergencies, and you have insured your income with life insurance. *If you keep needing what you want, there will come a time you will want what you really need*- Ricky So.

This chapter will be incomplete if we fail to mention the four biggest emotions and mindset blocks which stand in the way of taking and action and succeeding with our financial goals.

✓ Having a comfort zone: A comfort zone is one of the biggest challenges you would have to overcome if you have one. The only way you can change your financial life for good is to start being comfortable with feeling uncomfortable. The wealthy are aware of this. They know that evolving and growing comfort zone is key to success. You become very capable of dealing with fear the moment comfort becomes a big factor in your life. Don't be angry that you don't have money now, don't be frustrated that you can't get your wants. Let that feeling push you to make that success move.

✓ Doubt: The rich and the poor have an equal share of this. What makes the difference is what you are able to do, the decision you are able to take even when you are faced with doubt. The solution to acting despite your doubt is understanding that variety is another way to view uncertainty. When doubt comes, don't retreat to your comfort zone. Move forward, seek new opportunities and possibilities.

✓ Worry: I once heard this statement from someone; *the rich worry a lot because they have stocks everywhere.* Well, I don't know how true that is based on the next point below. I think it may be so. But wouldn't you rather worry in your own mansion or penthouse than to worriless in a rented apartment? Dealing with your finances can cause a lot of worries. We stress about having enough, making more money, losing money, and we also worry about taxes, business ideas, and profits, investments, etc. How can you deal with the stress that follows? Take action! Keep taking action.

✓ Inconvenience: We really need to face the fact here. Sometimes, being rich is not always going to be convenient. And it wouldn't be easy also. Much effort than you think is needed to change your financial status. Life will always be hard but you should be willing to take the hard road, and things would become easy. Get out of that comfort zone, make hard choices. It isn't going to be easy. But I tell you that every inch of discomfort you experience would be replaced with numerous satisfaction as time goes on.

No-one is free from the financial rat race. Even professionals who are up in their game are gaining a lot at the end of the month. They also face some obstacles.

First, they are isolated because people feel that they don't *need help*. The truth remains that it is hard to build wealth on your own. You are vulnerable alone, and you may never reach your fullest potential when you are not with the right people. In today's changing financial environment it's very pivotal than ever before to have the support of a mastermind group. They are also worn-out by fear like others also. They are faced with the fear of failure (a very prevalent one), fear of debt, fear of success and fear of the unknown.

The choice is yours. Below, I have listed four financial categories you currently fall into. However, it left to you to decide today about which category you want to work towards achieving.

1. Financial Crisis:

You have no savings

Live from mouth to mouth

Spend more than you earn.

Consistently rely on credit to get

through.

Have more than two credit cards and use one to pay the other.

2. Financial stability:

You live within your means.

You have sufficient savings to cover for three months of your basic living expenses which include mortgage/rent, car, debts, rates, water, insurance, utilities, and food.

Three months is measured stability because that is how long it takes the average person to find another job if they lose theirs. If you go with the thought that it may take more than 3 months to secure a job, then you would have to increase the amount of months savings to match.

3. Financial Security:

You have sufficient savings or capital invested (i.e., property and/or shares) to provide you an annual income to cover 12 months of your basic living expenses.

4. Financial Freedom/ independence:

This is when you have financial capital invested to the extent that you can survive without ever having to work again. You have an infinite income which allows you to live your dreams without limitations and you can afford to get something without asking *"how much is that?"*

The choice is yours; Face the hurdles of financial restraints now, overcome them, stick to your plan, make sure you achieve them. Then sit back, relax, enjoy your retirement and live a stress-free life.

Paths To Financial Freedom

So you must have made that decision to take control of your financial future and freedom. Or are you yet to do that? But how are you supposed to achieve this? Especially with countless promises and products which *guarantee your success.* It becomes very easy for you to give up even without starting. Just take your time to go to the search engine and type in make money from home or make money online. You would be bombarded with some get rich quick schemes with fake promises. Is there any way to be financially free? Do we have any path to financial independence?

We should start first by having the mentality of the rich. Research has it that the most influential part of one's life is between ages 4 and 18. Between these age brackets, we become exposed to information we will ever use as a person. Printed in our hearts and minds are the guidelines of how the world works, how we can make our futures and the right way to live for everyone or most people. You are taught how to work hard, get things done by yourself and interact with other people doing the same thing. You become rooted in the rat race as you are thought how to be a successful employee for the rest of your life.

The idea of being a good employee is not a bad idea. But definitely, it is not a path of victory or conquest. Sure that feeling that people get when they land the job they want or get that promotion they've been waiting for is incomparable. However, when you become an employee, you become tied to this never-ending ladder full of steps for you to climb. You will be very happy when everything comes together for you every few years. You go to work for a few more years to feel good. Then eventually you are given the *honor* to retire, take a pay cut, and live off a small salary until you die. The number one path to financial freedom is to *hate* your job. Yes! Hate it. Don't be satisfied with it. Tell me isn't it boring. Getting up each day, going to work, coming back, it sounds monotonous.

Your financial freedom comes when you are able to save, invest money wisely and accumulate assets for the future through carefully planned strategies. Paths to financial freedom include; planning, gaining financial knowledge, having the discipline to practice things that need to be done and believing in yourself. Just as I have mentioned earlier your desire to achieve financial freedom is the generating power of ACTION. Success will only come if you do something you believe in.

First, you have to set your financial goals. Your financial goals like every other goal can be classified as Short term, midterm, and Long term. Make sure your goals are realistic. You should learn to treat yourself as a business manager, responsible for managing your financial resources. To be successful financially, you really need to know where you are going and how you will get there. Setting goals are as important as deciding to be financially free. You need to be able to transform these ideas and dreams into reality. You can't just sit back and hope the money will fall from the sky (although that would be nice!) Take time to strategize for the future. A realistic goal is a goal which can be measured. You must be able to say that at this time, I should have $20,000 in my account.

In addition to the above, you should develop your own personal money management program. Well, how can you do this? Educate yourself. Read books, try schemes. Meet with other professionals, financial planners, and banks. When developing your personal money management program, you are expected to live within your income. Know how much you spend, your financial responsibilities and how to control expenses.

Next, you develop an effective savings plan. Your savings objectives will be dependent on your current economic circumstances. The world's most financially successful people make saving a priority. Just putting away the smallest amount of money each month into your savings account can perform wonders for you and your family. This habit of continuously investing in savings to build wealth over time have been practiced by most of the successful people in the world. When you plan your savings, you stop impulsive buying drastically. We all know that feeling of buying something on a whim. It is exciting, and it leaves us wanting for more. The culture of mass consumption has made most of us fall victim of the temptation of buying impulsively and making unplanned purchases. Behavior like this is very dangerous for our bank accounts. Sadly, we know this, but we still fall into that trap. People that are financially stable plan their purchases weigh the pros and cons of all their buying decisions.

Another thing is to learn to invest wisely. Your goal is to increase your wealth over time and to get the best possible return from the money you invest. It is important for you here to always take into account the prevailing economy. Each type of investment comes with its level of risk and consequences. You should understand this properly. You should read and analyze all documents given to you in the bank and all the fine print before signing anything and, only after you have sought professional help. Furthermore, you may want to consider if the investment is suitable for you or whether it is the right time to invest. You should also think of how much you can safely afford to invest? The benefits and risk involved. Will the investment provide a reasonable return for the amount of money invested? You should also consider; your assets and liabilities, current interest rates and cost involved. Nevertheless, you should consider the following:

- Your assets and liabilities
- Current interest rates and the costs involved

- Fully understanding the benefits and the consequences of effective credit use.
- Investigate all sources and always look for the best deals. This means that you shouldn't be satisfied with what you are getting from your stockbroker. There is nothing bad in seeking advice from multiple stockbrokers.
- Make sure you deal with well-established firms and qualified people
- Never be late in repaying loans.

It would be so unprofessional of me to conclude this chapter without making mention of the online aspect of financial freedom and how you can be able to tap into this resource. Not in this day where we have Bitcoin Millionaires and the like. Many individuals have created financial freedom through building business offline and the traditional way, like opening up a retail store, or buying real estate, selling insurance the list really goes on to infinite ways it has been done before. But the reality remains stagnant. You can start a virtual online empire which will skyrocket you to financial freedom faster than any of the traditional means you know. Most people have bad taste in their mouth when they hear anything online like network marketing because of all the failure stories they hear. The truth remains that they are just stories. Most times people fail in this industry because they do not stick with it long enough to see that it works.You are sticking with the plan. Remember? You must have that resilience to remain through the good and bad times in order to prosper. And this goes for every kind of business you may want to venture into. When it comes to having an online business empire, first you must be able to keep up with technology and have a real mentor to teach you. Definitely, you will hit bumps on the road to success, but that is not a good reason for you to give up on your dreams and goals.

Today, more millionaires are coming out of the network marketing industry today than any other industry you have out there. You are the only one who can make the decision to achieve financial freedom. Get yourself familiarized with your *computer.*The computer here doesn't necessarily mean the device. But any instrument you intend to use, phones, applications, bitcoin, etc. Furthermore, you need to take calculated risk also. With just a click you can lose millions and gain millions too. Think of this as a chess game. You make specific moves to keep away from the checkmate. The wiser your decisions are and the faster you take action, the faster you will achieve financial freedom.

I would highlight some practical paths to success and how to get started. Don't look at this as a repeat of the points above but rather a reinforcement. In mapping out your financial freedom path, you must be:

- Be accountable and responsible: The very step on the path of financial success is for you to accept responsibility. Only you are in control of your financial future, and every choice you make would definitely havean impact. Irrespective of your age, education or background. You need to ask yourself questions that matter; are you completing your own financial aid paperwork? Are you in charge or do you have equal input in paying your bills and managing your finances? Do you do thorough research before you make any big purchase (like a car or computer)? When you become involved from the start, you become aware of your responsibilities and obligations. You also need to ask yourself these questions; if you lend money or enter into another financial commitment, do you always understand your rights and responsibilities? Are the *terms* and *conditions* gibberish? Do you find business news boring?

Being responsible also involves paying your debts on time. When you pay late, do you know it has a great effect on you? You know that the credit bureaus are always quick to compile your report and also calculate your score. When you pay late, your credit score drops. This credit score is usually based on; how you pay bills on time, the total amount of debt you have and how close to your credit limit that amount is, the number of accounts you recently opened, the number of recent inquiries about your credit score, the different type of accounts currently opened, the length of time you have been building credit. Your creditors will grade you on these and even more. Therefore, put off the coat of irresponsibility, carelessness, and sloppiness now!

- Plot your course of action: This is where I remind you that you have to be specific, being specific isn't the only thing, but you also need to be realistic. Most importantly you need to WRITE DOWN YOUR GOALS. When you write down your goals, you would be able to keep records and mark off key milestones as you achieve them. When you review your goals, and you record your progress, you motivate yourself. After you have been able to identify your goals, you map out how you are going to achieve them. Several questions are needed to be answered; like how much income do you have available? How much will you need to achieve your goal (this is where you have to be as realistic as possible)? Do you have any other goal you need to finish before you start planning? Financial freedom is a journey where you'll need total focus.

- Understand your income: Let's picture this. You've just been offered a job at a local firm. They've offered you 40 hours per week starting from $15 per hour; this means that you'll be taking home $600 (40X15) dollars a week right?

Wrong!

If you have no understanding of your income, I advise that you get that report, document or anything you need to get from your employee.

In understanding your income, you need to know that there are numerous deductions take from your gross pay (the hours multiplied by your hourly wage). What you receive after all these deductions have been made is the net pay. Standard deductions are; federal income tax, social security, and Medicare. Other deductions include: state taxes, additional retirement contributions, health insurance, cafeteria plan benefits, wage garnishment, agreed automatic withholdings, etc. Note that all these charges are individually distinct.

- Open a checking account: What does a checking account do? Why do I have to open it? It should be noted that this point is just a suggestion, just like every other thing in this book. It must not be taken hook line and sinker. A checking account is a very secure place to keep your money. Not that all other accounts are less secure, but it helps you track your money. What a checking account does is that it creates a paper trail which would help you in knowing how much money is available to spend and how much you have spent. But before you open a checking account, you must do thorough research to find a bank or credit union which provides an account which suits your needs. And just as I have mentioned. If you don't know everything about it, don't go into it. We have three common types of account; the standard, special and interest-bearing account. We have some special banks which offer "free" checking accounts and other enticements specifically for students, etc. The check register is also an important element in your checking account. You should record all transaction, deposit, withdrawals, deduction, etc. For example, you have; cash deposit-the checks are written, ATM or debit card transactions should also be monitored.

- Start saving and investing money. If you don't have a savings account, I would advise that you should open one now! I should also emphasize here that you should pay yourself first! Depositing money into a savings account should take priority over any additional spending. As you pay your monthly bills, make sure to set money aside to deposit into your savings. You can also ask your bank to automatically transfer money from your checking to your savings once, twice or thrice a month. You can also request a direct deposit from your employer for a portion of your paycheck to be deposited into your savings.

- Borrow smart: Whenever you are considering taking any loan. You should consider; the interest rate, additional fees, and down payments. However, there are some additional guidelines to help you determine whether or not to borrow money; first, housing expenses should not exceed 33 percent of what you have as gross income. A lot of lending institutions look at this factor in determining your loan eligibility. Furthermore, loan installment payments which include auto and student loans, as well as credit cards, should not exceed a combined total of 20 percent of what appears to be your gross income. Finally, save money and have at least 6-12 months of emergency savings.

Finance gurus, stock brokers, employees, and even employers keep talking about becoming financially free. However, the truth remains that if you want to become financially free, you must be ready to take passive income as serious as the major source of income. I know this may sound too serious, but that is the truth. Passive income is not really passive; it is a serious aspect of your financial life that you should give all attention also.

There are four major sources which can serve as that extra well of passive income.

- ✓ The Earned income. This is the money earned from your time and energy. People have those side hustle which helps them get some extra income.

- ✓ The portfolio income is the kind of income you receive from extra dividends and capital gains which comes from owning stocks and other mutual funds.

- ✓ Leverage income is generated when one particular occupation or pursuit gives you more money larger than that captured audience. Let's take for example you plan to give a lecture to 200 people, but only 20 arrive, you stock their heads with so many principles that they demand other things (materials) meant for the 200. You've earned much with the smaller group.

✓ You may want to consider passive income as this side hustle which involves investment, and it produces cash like every other business transaction

We can definitely tell from the above that earned incomes puts you in the position to pay your bills, but it would also sustain you until you're able to get such promotions and raises. That is why you shouldn't limit your income by just putting all your eggs in one basket.

So with passive income, you would be able to create that compound flow of income. Increase your passive income, and you'll be able to lift yourself out of every financial problem to become financially free.

The following are some suggestions on how you can begin to make some passive income.

- License a patent
- Cash flow positive real estate
- Automated fulfillment websites
- Pay for use items
- Build a successful business
- Become an Author: Copyrighting materials that earn royalties, such as books or e-books, especially is a strong way entrepreneurs create passive income.
- We should know that passive income does not necessarily mean that there is no involvement on your end. Creating passive income streams often involves a large

investment up-front, but in the end, it requires little or no interaction.

- Also, just because you make an earned income now (opposed to passive income) does not mean that you should quit your day job and open up a quarter car wash. To start building passive income streams, you will likely need to keep making an earned income in order to convert that income into passive income by purchasing rental properties, etc. Active income can actually be extremely beneficial in creating more passive income.

- Once your passive income is greater than your expenses, you can make the decision to stop making an earned income and live the rest of your life financially free.

Conclusion

Thank you for reading this book and I really hope you enjoyed it and have learnt that anybody can use the stock market amongst other things to become financially free and finally be free of the burden that is debt. While it may seem I am against active investing, I am certainly not and I do myself invest in an active manner on top of my index funds. However, this requires much more work and research and if you are interested in taking that route I would highly recommend educating yourself further on active investing in the Stock Market with books, courses and potentially even a mentor. I personally have some books on active investing and am in the process of producing more. But, for the average person who doesn't want to dedicate hours and hours to research and education I wholeheartedly recommend index funds and passive investing as the easiest way to build a substantial nest egg for your retirement or early retirement if that is your goal.

Also, please remember the Stock Market is one way to build wealth, however, there are many more ways to also build wealth. For example starting a business and then reinvesting profits either back in the business or into the Stock Market and continuing to let it all compound over decades adds even more power to Compound Interest. I would recommend not becoming narrow minded and researching all the ways to build wealth whether that be through "Active" income, "Passive" income or investments such as the Stock Market and Real Estate. We live in an ever changing world so always be prepared to adapt. I don't imagine for one second that our grandparents believed they would be able to send a "text message" let alone video call anyone from anywhere in the world within seconds. The world is always changing and as individuals we need to be able to keep up with the ever changing world.

Anyways, I hope this book has opened your eyes to how lucrative the Stock Market can be and how simple investing can be with the power of index funds, passive investing and compound interest. Here's to your success!

www.ingramcontent.com/pod-product-compliance
Lightning Source LLC
Chambersburg PA
CBHW072255210326
41458CB00074B/1740